Goodbye Gemini: Reclaiming My Identity Finding the Truth

The Companion Journal

Sharelle McNair

Copyright

Goodbye Gemini: Reclaiming My Identity, Finding the Truth

The Companion Journal

©2025 Sharelle McNair

Published in Hampton, VA, by Fruition Publishing Concierge Services®. Fruition Publishing Concierge Services® is a division of Alesha Brown, LLC. Fruition Publishing Concierge Services® can bring authors to your live event. For more information or to book an event, visit Fruition Publishing Concierge Services® at:

www.FruitionPublishing.com

ISBN: 978-1-954486-62-1 eBook

ISBN: 978-1-954486-63-8 Paperback

Library Of Congress Control Number: 978-1-954486-63-8

Contents

Dedication

I cannot move forward without first thanking My Father, The Good Father, My God, My Lord, My King, My Everything! You are THE reason I am alive. You are what motivates me the most. You give me my drive. You made me everything that I am. Your grace and love for me have been unshakable, even when I was far away. You would come for me even when my face was turned and my head was down. You are "The Truth" of my life.

You have spoken to me and answered me in so many ways that my life would be absolutely nothing without you. I love You and I hunger for all things You. I want to publicly glorify You to the world by proclaiming to it that my life, my lessons, my success, my joy, my intelligence, my family, my gifts, my homes, my bank account, my sanity, and everything that makes up Sharelle, would not at all be possible without You. I thank you for the blood of Jesus that covers my life and all that surrounds me. Use me, Father, how you choose. Use these words as you choose. Have your way in my life continually, for I have been running and disobedient for too long. Allow my readers to experience You in ways unheard of. You are The Great I Am! I am because You Are.

To my sons Romell and Aakell, I love you to the moon and back. You two boys have truly been a joy to raise. You both are so wonderful, so fun, so funny, so kind, so smart, and I love having you in my life. God made both of you perfect for me. God has already told me some of who you two are to Him, so I am more than excited to see how you both fulfill God's will and purpose for your life. I am here to rock with you both all the way until the end. Mama and Daddy will always make sure you are straight. I celebrate you, my young kings, and I dedicate you both to the good Lord. Remember, your middle names are Messiah and Prince to honor our big brother Jesus, the Christ of Nazareth. You are joint heirs, God's sons. You are my babies.

I want to thank all my family, especially Mom, Dad, and my brothers, for doing your best to make me the princess of the household. Thanks for assisting, encouraging, disciplining, supporting, laughing, playing, talking, schooling, driving, dancing, screaming, hugging, loving, praying, and so much more for me throughout the years. I love you all dearly. This is for all of us. I will make you all more than proud. I love you Ashlynn, Alonni and Eri. You three are my girls and auntie got you forever! To the Mann and McNair, Jasper, and Bailey family: I love every single one of you, and I hope this is just a piece of the many wonderful things God is going to do in our family legacy.

I want to thank my Spiritual Parents, Pastor Brad and Quiana Johnson, and all of my spiritual family and dear friends over the years for continually praying for me, and loving on my family by: inviting us to your homes, cooking us dinner, giving us rides, babysitting the boys, allowing me to vent, throwing us parties, buying us clothes, giving us furniture, giving us advice, covering us in our weaknesses, calling us, letting us sleep on your couch, loving us even in our worst moments, traveling with us, keeping our secrets, counseling us, interceding for us, and all the other many ways you all have continually contributed to our lives. I am forever grateful. I pray that God blesses all of you beyond your wildest dreams. I pray I have been as much of a blessing to you as you have been to my family and me.

Finally, I want to thank everyone who has contributed to my life good and bad, from childhood to now. Your presence and contributions to the fabric of my life have shaped and molded me into the woman that I am today. There are really too many of you to name, but each of you has added valuable pieces to me finally being able to walk in my true God-given identity.

Journal With Me

How to Use This Journal

From the Publisher:

This journal is your sacred space. Use it to reflect, release, and reconnect with God as you explore each chapter of Goodbye Gemini. After reading each chapter, use the journal prompts to dig deeper into your thoughts, beliefs, and healing process.

There is no right or wrong way to use this journal. Find a quiet space, take your time, and be honest. Use the lined pages to write freely and the blank pages to pray, sketch, or dream. Let this be a tool of transformation as you let go of the lies and embrace God's truth about who you are.

Remember: this is not homework—it's healing work. Let the Holy Spirit guide your pen.

From the Author:

These are some writing prompts that I want you to really stop, think about, pray about, and be open with God about. If the question doesn't apply, move on and save for later.

Go to your quiet place and allow yourself to reflect. Let the Spirit speak. Cry, laugh, scream, and don't forget to have fun! I pray you are healed from the inside out, in Jesus' name!

Chapter 1

Goodbye Gemini

1) Before reading Chapter One, did you believe in horoscopes/zodiac signs? Why?

_____

_____

_____

_____

_____

_____

_____

_____

_____

GOODBYE GEMINI (continued)

2) What does your sign say about you and your personality/characteristics? Do you agree?

_____

_____

_____

_____

_____

_____

_____

_____

_____

_____

_____

_____

_____

_____

_____

_____

_____

_____

GOODBYE GEMINI (continued)

3) Are there any experiences in your life that bring out specific personality traits? Do you have triggers?

_____
_____
_____
_____
_____
_____
_____
_____
_____
_____
_____
_____
_____
_____
_____
_____
_____

GOODBYE GEMINI (continued)

4) Search the Bible for scriptures about your personality traits. What does the Word say about those characteristics?

_____

_____

_____

_____

_____

_____

_____

_____

_____

_____

_____

_____

_____

_____

_____

_____

_____

GOODBYE GEMINI (continued)

2 Corinthians 5:17 (NLT) says: "This means that anyone who belongs to Christ has become a new person. The old life is gone; a new life has begun!"

5) What does that mean for your life? What would letting go of the old life look like?

_____

_____

_____

_____

_____

_____

_____

_____

_____

_____

_____

_____

GOODBYE GEMINI (continued)

6) Is there something else you believed about yourself that you no longer need to believe?

Write about it.

_____

_____

_____

_____

_____

_____

_____

_____

_____

_____

_____

_____

_____

_____

_____

_____

GOODBYE GEMINI (continued)

7) Is there an idol that you worship—something that you love, dedicate time and money to, or place on the throne of your heart—that takes God's place?

Are you willing to let it go?

_____

_____

_____

_____

_____

_____

_____

_____

_____

_____

_____

_____

_____

_____

GOODBYE GEMINI (continued)

8) Write this down and fill in the blank with your sign.

"Goodbye _____." Say it aloud.

---

9) **Now mark it out, write *Hello,* and fill in the blank with your name.**

   "Hello _____*."* **Say it out aloud. Close your eyes. Say it again aloud.**

Who do you see? What is she doing?

Prayer Reflection-Chapter 1

Prayer Reflection

Use this page to write a prayer or listen to what God is saying to you in this chapter.

_____

_____

_____

_____

_____

_____

_____

_____

Scripture Reflection-
Chapter 1

Scripture Reflection

Use these scriptures for deeper reflection, prayer, and revelation.

- *2 Corinthians 5:17 – You are a new creation in Christ.*

- *Galatians 2:20 – Crucified with Christ, now living by faith.*

- *Isaiah 43:18, 19 – Forget the former things; I am doing a new thing.*

Scripture Reflection-Chapter 1 (continued)

Scripture Reflection (continued)

Use these scriptures for deeper reflection, prayer, and revelation.

- *Romans 12:2 – Be transformed by the renewing of your mind.*

- *Colossians 2:8 – Don't be captured by philosophies not based on Christ.*

Chapter 2

The God Box

1) What is your definition of God?

Does your understanding come from what you have been taught, what you have read, or what you have experienced?

_____

_____

_____

_____

_____

_____

_____

_____

THE GOD BOX (continued)

2) How does it feel to hear that you cannot earn salvation?

Have you been trying to do good so you will be forgiven? Do you believe you are forgiven already?

_____

_____

_____

_____

_____

_____

_____

_____

_____

_____

_____

_____

_____

_____

THE GOD BOX (continued)

3) Do you desire to know the God of Heaven? Is there anything about Jesus Christ that you do not understand or do not believe?

What is holding you back from fully experiencing the presence of the Holy Spirit?

_____

_____

_____

_____

_____

_____

_____

_____

_____

_____

_____

_____

_____

_____

_____

THE GOD BOX (continued)

4) Worship* means *to* "honor or show reverence for a divine being, supernatural power, or to regard with great or extravagant respect, honor, or devotion (*Merriam-Webster.com Dictionary*, s.v. "worship," accessed December 1, 2023, https://www.merriam-webster.com/dictionary/worship)."

How do you worship?

---

* Merriam-Webster.com Dictionary, s.v. "worship," accessed December 1, 2023, https://www.merriam-webster.com/dictionary/worship.

THE GOD BOX (continued)

5) Take a look at what you spend the most money on. What do you spend the most time thinking about and doing? What or who would you die for?

Who or what is it that you worship? Do you need to change your worship?

_____

_____

_____

_____

_____

_____

_____

_____

_____

_____

_____

_____

_____

_____

_____

THE GOD BOX (continued)

6) Ask The Lord, "How do you want me to worship you, My King? I want to worship you."

What is God saying to you? Write it down.

_____

_____

_____

_____

_____

_____

_____

_____

_____

_____

_____

_____

_____

_____

THE GOD BOX (continued)

7) Close your eyes and imagine yourself free in worship in Heaven. Write about what you see.

_____

_____

_____

_____

_____

_____

_____

_____

_____

_____

_____

_____

_____

_____

_____

_____

_____

Prayer Reflection-Chapter 2

Prayer Reflection

Use this page to write a prayer or listen to what God is saying to you in this chapter.

_____

_____

_____

_____

_____

_____

_____

_____

Scripture Reflection- Chapter 2

Scripture Reflection

Use these scriptures for deeper reflection, prayer, and revelation.

- *John 4:23, 24 – True worshipers worship in spirit and truth.*

- *Exodus 20:3, 4 – You shall have no other gods before Me.*

- *Romans 10:9, 10 – Believe in your heart and confess with your mouth.*

Scripture Reflection-Chapter 2 (continued)

Scripture Reflection (continued)

Use these scriptures for deeper reflection, prayer, and revelation.

- *Isaiah 55:8, 9 – His thoughts are higher than ours.*

- *Psalm 139:1–6 – He knows everything about you.*

Chapter 3

I Want To Love Myself, But I Can't...

1) What have people said about you or to you that has made you feel inferior? Do you behave differently because of their words? How? Why?

Allow yourself to be vulnerable and honest. Write about it.

_____

_____

_____

_____

_____

_____

_____

_____

I WANT TO LOVE MYSELF, BUT
I CAN'T... (continued)

2) Now ask God what He says about those things.

Does God's word agree with those negative thoughts? What does God say about you?

_____

_____

_____

_____

_____

_____

_____

_____

_____

_____

_____

_____

_____

_____

I WANT TO LOVE MYSELF, BUT
I CAN'T... (continued)

3) Is it difficult to receive the good things God has to say about you? Why? Write about it.

_____

_____

_____

_____

_____

_____

_____

_____

_____

_____

_____

_____

_____

_____

_____

_____

I WANT TO LOVE MYSELF, BUT I CAN'T... (continued)

4) How do you feel about your looks? Do your looks affect your confidence?

_____
_____
_____
_____
_____
_____
_____
_____
_____
_____
_____
_____
_____
_____
_____
_____
_____
_____

I WANT TO LOVE MYSELF, BUT
I CAN'T... (continued)

5) Where does your confidence come from? When do you feel most valued?

_____

_____

_____

_____

_____

_____

_____

_____

_____

_____

_____

_____

_____

_____

_____

_____

_____

I WANT TO LOVE MYSELF, BUT
I CAN'T... (continued)

**6) Write down every negative idea about yourself.
Cross it out and write NO.**

How do these negative ideas make you feel?

_____

_____

_____

_____

_____

_____

_____

_____

_____

_____

_____

_____

_____

_____

_____

I WANT TO LOVE MYSELF, BUT
I CAN'T... (continued)

7) Make a list of everything you love about yourself. Write Yes beside it.

Will you say Yes to the best you?

_____

_____

_____

_____

_____

_____

_____

_____

_____

_____

_____

_____

_____

_____

_____

I WANT TO LOVE MYSELF, BUT
I CAN'T... (continued)

8) Are you willing to dust off the dirt that has been thrown on you, or that you threw on yourself?

What does your clean slate look like, sound like, and feel like? Write about it.

_____

_____

_____

_____

_____

_____

_____

_____

_____

_____

_____

_____

_____

_____

Prayer Reflection-Chapter 3

Prayer Reflection

Use this page to write a prayer or listen to what God is saying to you in this chapter.

_____

_____

_____

_____

_____

_____

_____

Scripture Reflection-
Chapter 3

Scripture Reflection

Use these scriptures for deeper reflection, prayer, and revelation.

- *Psalm 139:13, 14 – Fearfully and wonderfully made.*

- *Ephesians 2:10 – You are God's workmanship.*

- *Romans 8:1 – No condemnation for those in Christ.*

Scripture Reflection-Chapter 3 (continued)

Scripture Reflection (continued)

Use these scriptures for deeper reflection, prayer, and revelation.

- *2 Corinthians 10:5 – Take every thought captive.*

- *Zephaniah 3:17 – He rejoices over you with singing.*

Chapter 4

Daddy's Lock

1) Are you close to your earthly daddy? Why or why not?

Are there any steps you can take to build a closer relationship with your dad?

_____

_____

_____

_____

_____

_____

_____

_____

DADDY'S LOCK (continued)

2) Write down the ways your dad has disappointed you. How do these actions make you feel?

Are you willing to forgive him?

_____

_____

_____

_____

_____

_____

_____

_____

_____

_____

_____

_____

_____

_____

_____

_____

DADDY'S LOCK (continued)

3) Write down the good memories of your father.

How do these memories make you feel?

_____

_____

_____

_____

_____

_____

_____

_____

_____

_____

_____

_____

_____

_____

_____

_____

_____

_____

_____

DADDY'S LOCK (continued)

4) In what ways do you feel you are similar to your father? In what ways are you different?

What have you learned from your daddy?

_____

_____

_____

_____

_____

_____

_____

_____

_____

_____

_____

_____

_____

_____

_____

_____

_____

DADDY'S LOCK (continued)

5) Now focus on your Heavenly Father. Say aloud, "You are my Heavenly Father."

How does that make you feel? Is it comfortable and easy to say?

Write about it. And repeat that statement as much as you can until you believe it.

_____

_____

_____

_____

_____

_____

_____

_____

_____

_____

_____

DADDY'S LOCK (continued)

6) In what ways has God the Father been a father to you that you recollect?

What would you desire from your Heavenly Father? What does your relationship to The Father look like?

_____

_____

_____

_____

_____

_____

_____

_____

_____

_____

_____

_____

_____

_____

_____

_____

DADDY'S LOCK (continued)

7) In what ways has the Heavenly Father stepped in where your earthly father lacked?

_____

_____

_____

_____

_____

_____

_____

_____

_____

_____

_____

_____

_____

_____

_____

_____

_____

DADDY'S LOCK (continued)

8) Write a letter to your earthly father saying everything you want to say.

Next, write a letter to the Heavenly Father saying everything you want to say.

_____

_____

_____

_____

_____

_____

_____

_____

_____

_____

_____

_____

_____

_____

Prayer Reflection-Chapter 4

Prayer Reflection

Use this page to write a prayer or listen to what God is saying to you in this chapter.

_____

_____

_____

_____

_____

_____

_____

_____

Scripture Reflection- Chapter 4

Scripture Reflection

Use these scriptures for deeper reflection, prayer, and revelation.

- *Psalm 27:10 – When my father and mother forsake me...*

- *Matthew 6:9 – Our Father who art in heaven.*

- *Luke 15:20 – The father ran to meet his son.*

Scripture Reflection-Chapter 4 (continued)

Scripture Reflection (continued)

Use these scriptures for deeper reflection, prayer, and revelation.

- *1 John 3:1 – See what great love the Father has.*

- *Hebrews 12:6 – The Lord disciplines those He loves.*

Chapter 5

Mama's Key

1) **What is something your mama told you that you believe about yourself? Does this affect you positively or negatively?**

Write about it and how it makes you feel.

_____

_____

_____

_____

_____

_____

_____

_____

MAMA'S KEY (continued)

2) Are you close to your mom? Do you desire to be closer? What can you do to build a closer bond with your mother?

_____

_____

_____

_____

_____

_____

_____

_____

_____

_____

_____

_____

_____

_____

_____

_____

MAMA'S KEY (continued)

3) What are some experiences with your mom that you despise? Do you have some hidden resentment towards your mom?

Write a letter to your mom about how she disappointed you, made you angry, made you cry, or caused you pain in other ways.

_____

_____

_____

_____

_____

_____

_____

_____

_____

_____

_____

_____

_____

_____

MAMA'S KEY (continued)

4) Are you able to be honest with your mom? Or are you forced to be inauthentic with your mom to save her ego or reputation?

Write about it and be completely transparent.

_____

_____

_____

_____

_____

_____

_____

_____

_____

_____

_____

_____

_____

_____

MAMA'S KEY (continued)

5) If your mother were gone tomorrow, what would you miss about her?

Write it down. With that in mind, will you choose to cherish her presence now?

_____

_____

_____

_____

_____

_____

_____

_____

_____

_____

_____

_____

_____

_____

MAMA'S KEY (continued)

6) Is there anything that you do that is similar to your mom? What did she pass down that you can thank her for?

Write her a thank-you letter.

_____

_____

_____

_____

_____

_____

_____

_____

_____

_____

_____

_____

_____

_____

MAMA'S KEY (continued)

7) What are some things you never knew about your mom that you would want to know or talk about?

Write it down and use these as conversation starters.

_____

_____

_____

_____

_____

_____

_____

_____

_____

_____

_____

_____

_____

_____

_____

_____

_____

_____

_____

MAMA'S KEY (continued)

Psalms 27:10 (NLT) says: "Even if my father and mother abandon me, the Lord will hold me close."

8) Can you see where the Lord was holding you close, filling in where your parents lacked? Write about it.

_____

_____

_____

_____

_____

_____

_____

_____

_____

_____

_____

_____

_____

_____

Prayer Reflection-Chapter 5

Prayer Reflection

Use this page to write a prayer or listen to what God says to you in this chapter.

_____

_____

_____

_____

_____

_____

_____

_____

Scripture Reflection- Chapter 5

Scripture Reflection

Use these scriptures for deeper reflection, prayer, and revelation.

- *Proverbs 31:28, 29 – Her children rise and call her blessed.*

- *Exodus 20:12 – Honor your father and mother.*

- *Psalm 34:18 – The Lord is near to the brokenhearted.*

Scripture Reflection-Chapter 5 (continued)

Scripture Reflection (continued)

Use these scriptures for deeper reflection, prayer, and revelation.

- *Isaiah 66:13 – As a mother comforts her child, so I will comfort you.*

- *Proverbs 15:1 – A gentle answer turns away wrath.*

Chapter 6

TWERKING, NAKED, and ASHAMED

1) What is your viewpoint about sex (premarital sex, casual sex, adultery, marital sex, etc.)? Examine where your viewpoint came from.

Does your viewpoint match what the Word of God says about sex?

_____

_____

_____

_____

_____

_____

_____

_____

TWERKING, NAKED, and ASHAMED (continued)

2) Do you enjoy sex? Do you dislike sex? Why?

Be honest and write to God about your sexual life and sexual encounters.

_____

_____

_____

_____

_____

_____

_____

_____

_____

_____

_____

_____

_____

_____

TWERKING, NAKED, and ASHAMED (continued)

3) If God required you to abstain from sex, could you? Would it be hard?

_____

_____

_____

_____

_____

_____

_____

_____

_____

_____

_____

_____

_____

_____

_____

_____

4) If you have had sexual relations that you are ashamed of, do you receive God's forgiveness for your mistakes and choices? Do you forgive yourself?

_____

_____

_____

_____

_____

_____

_____

_____

_____

_____

_____

_____

_____

_____

_____

_____

_____

_____

TWERKING, NAKED, and ASHAMED (continued)

5) Do you enjoy pornography? What is it satisfying in you that you are lacking? Why do you need it? Are you willing to let it go?

Write about it.

_____

_____

_____

_____

_____

_____

_____

_____

_____

_____

_____

_____

_____

_____

_____

_____

6) What are some ways you can help shield and protect the youth in your life (children, nieces, nephews, siblings, students, etc.) from exposure to sexual experiences and encounters?

_____

_____

_____

_____

_____

_____

_____

_____

_____

_____

_____

_____

_____

TWERKING, NAKED, and ASHAMED (continued)

7) What was your first sexual encounter? Are you healed from that experience?

_____

_____

_____

_____

_____

_____

_____

_____

_____

_____

_____

_____

_____

_____

_____

_____

_____

_____

TWERKING, NAKED, and ASHAMED (continued)

8) Are there any secrets about your sexual life that you need to release?

Write about it to God.

_____

_____

_____

_____

_____

_____

_____

_____

_____

_____

_____

_____

_____

_____

TWERKING, NAKED, and ASHAMED (continued)

IF YOU HAVE BEEN A VICTIM OF MOLESTATION, RAPE, OR SEX TRAFFICKING, PLEASE SUBMIT THAT ABUSE TO GOD, AND SEEK PROFESSIONAL HELP SUCH AS THERAPY, COUNSELING, MEDICAL CARE AND REPORT THE CRIME TO THE POLICE.

Prayer Reflection-Chapter 6

Prayer Reflection

Use this page to write a prayer or listen to what God is saying to you in this chapter.

_____

_____

_____

_____

_____

_____

_____

_____

Scripture Reflection- Chapter 6

Scripture Reflection

Use these scriptures for deeper reflection, prayer, and revelation.

- *1 Corinthians 6:18–20 – Your body is a temple.*

- *John 8:10, 11 – Neither do I condemn you... go and sin no more.*

- *Romans 8:38, 39 – Nothing can separate us from His love.*

Scripture Reflection-Chapter 6 (continued)

Scripture Reflection (continued)

Use these scriptures for deeper reflection, prayer, and revelation.

- *1 Thessalonians 4:3–5 – God's will is for you to be holy.*

- *Isaiah 1:18 – Though your sins are like scarlet, they shall be white as snow.*

Chapter 7

I Love You Like A Sister

1) Do you have a sister or a close friend? Write about what they contribute to your life.

_____

_____

_____

_____

_____

_____

_____

_____

_____

I LOVE YOU LIKE A SISTER
(continued)

2) Are you the friend you want to be? How can you improve? What can you do better to love your friends?

_____

_____

_____

_____

_____

_____

_____

_____

_____

_____

_____

_____

_____

_____

_____

_____

I LOVE YOU LIKE A SISTER
(continued)

3) Are you a safe place for your sister/friend? Can your sister be vulnerable with you, and you be vulnerable with her?

It is time you have an honest conversation. What do you need to say?

_____

_____

_____

_____

_____

_____

_____

_____

_____

_____

_____

_____

_____

_____

I LOVE YOU LIKE A SISTER
(continued)

4) In what ways has your sibling disappointed you? In what way has your best friend let you down? Write about it. Do you forgive them?

_____

_____

_____

_____

_____

_____

_____

_____

_____

_____

_____

_____

_____

_____

_____

_____

_____

_____

I LOVE YOU LIKE A SISTER
(continued)

5) Is there anyone in your life that you underappreciate and or take for granted? Who is that person, and how can you show them your appreciation? Write a letter to that person.

_____

_____

_____

_____

_____

_____

_____

_____

_____

_____

_____

_____

_____

_____

_____

_____

I LOVE YOU LIKE A SISTER
(continued)

6) Is there a sister or close friend that you lost that you are still mourning? Write about the joyful memories you have of that person.

Will you allow God to comfort you in your pain?

_____

_____

_____

_____

_____

_____

_____

_____

_____

_____

_____

_____

_____

_____

I LOVE YOU LIKE A SISTER
(continued)

7) Be a big sister and write a letter of advice to a younger sister (actual or fictional). What would you tell her?

_____

_____

_____

_____

_____

_____

_____

_____

_____

_____

_____

_____

_____

_____

_____

_____

_____

Prayer Reflection-Chapter 7

Prayer Reflection

Use this page to write a prayer or listen to what God is saying to you in this chapter.

_____

_____

_____

_____

_____

_____

_____

_____

Scripture Reflection- Chapter 7

Scripture Reflection

Use these scriptures for deeper reflection, prayer, and revelation.

- *Proverbs 17:17 – A friend loves at all times.*

- *Ecclesiastes 4:9, 10 – Two are better than one...*

- *Romans 12:10 – Be devoted to one another in love.*

Scripture Reflection-Chapter 7 (continued)

Scripture Reflection (continued)

Use these scriptures for deeper reflection, prayer, and revelation.

- *John 15:13 – Greater love has no one than this...*

- *Philippians 2:4 – Look to the interests of others.*

Chapter 8

Don't Awaken Love Before Its Time-Wifehood Is Not For The Weak

1) Do you desire to be married? Why or why not?

_____

_____

_____

_____

_____

_____

_____

_____

_____

DON'T AWAKEN LOVE BEFORE ITS TIME- WIFEHOOD IS NOT FOR THE WEAK (continued)

2) What is a wife? What does your being a wife look like?

_____

_____

_____

_____

_____

_____

_____

_____

_____

_____

_____

_____

_____

_____

_____

_____

DON'T AWAKEN LOVE BEFORE ITS TIME- WIFEHOOD IS NOT FOR THE WEAK (continued)

3) What do you want your marriage to be and look like? Pray and write the vision of your marriage.

_____

_____

_____

_____

_____

_____

_____

_____

_____

_____

_____

_____

_____

_____

_____

DON'T AWAKEN LOVE BEFORE ITS TIME-WIFEHOOD IS NOT FOR THE WEAK (continued)

4) If you are already married, is your marriage thriving or suffering? Write a prayer to God about your marriage.

Let God speak to you about your marriage. What is He saying?

_____

_____

_____

_____

_____

_____

_____

_____

_____

_____

_____

_____

DON'T AWAKEN LOVE BEFORE ITS TIME-WIFEHOOD IS NOT FOR THE WEAK (continued)

5) What could you do differently in your marriage to make it better? What should you stop doing to make it better?

Write a plan of action to change your mind and actions and do something new.

_____
_____
_____
_____
_____
_____
_____
_____
_____
_____
_____
_____

DON'T AWAKEN LOVE BEFORE ITS TIME-WIFEHOOD IS NOT FOR THE WEAK (continued)

5) Are there any hidden traumas, pain, or secrets from previous relationships that are affecting your current marriage? Confess to the Lord what they are and write His response.

_____

_____

_____

_____

_____

_____

_____

_____

_____

_____

_____

_____

_____

DON'T AWAKEN LOVE BEFORE ITS TIME-WIFEHOOD IS NOT FOR THE WEAK (continued)

6) Are there any areas in your spouse's life that you ignored that you need to confront (minor or major)?

Write your spouse a letter and let them know what is going on. Then have a face-to-face conversation.

_____

_____

_____

_____

_____

_____

_____

_____

_____

_____

_____

_____

DON'T AWAKEN LOVE BEFORE ITS TIME-WIFEHOOD IS NOT FOR THE WEAK (continued)

7) In what ways do you feel most loved? What makes you feel neglected? What do you need more of from your spouse? What do you need your spouse to stop doing?

Write it to the Lord and then listen to the Lord. Then have the conversation with your spouse.

_____

_____

_____

_____

_____

_____

_____

_____

_____

_____

_____

DON'T AWAKEN LOVE BEFORE ITS TIME- WIFEHOOD IS NOT FOR THE WEAK (continued)

8) What is the assignment of your marriage? How is God going to use your marriage?

_____

_____

_____

_____

_____

_____

_____

_____

_____

_____

_____

_____

_____

DON'T AWAKEN LOVE BEFORE ITS TIME-WIFEHOOD IS NOT FOR THE WEAK (continued)

9) What do you know about marriage now that you wish you had known beforehand? What advice would you give to a dating or engaged couple?

_____

_____

_____

_____

_____

_____

_____

_____

_____

_____

_____

_____

_____

_____

Prayer Reflection-Chapter 8

Prayer Reflection

Use this page to write a prayer or listen to what God is saying to you in this chapter.

_____
_____
_____
_____
_____
_____
_____
_____

Scripture Reflection-
Chapter 8

Scripture Reflection

Use these scriptures for deeper reflection, prayer, and revelation.

- *Song of Songs 8:4 – Do not awaken love before its time.*

- *Ephesians 5:22–33 – Instructions for wives and husbands.*

- *1 Corinthians 13:4–7 – Love is patient, love is kind...*

Scripture Reflection-Chapter 8
(continued)

Scripture Reflection (continued)

Use these scriptures for deeper reflection, prayer, and revelation.

- ***Proverbs 18:22 – He who finds a wife finds a good thing.***

- ***Colossians 3:14 – Put on love, which binds all together.***

Chapter 9

Chapter 9- Roemelo And Prince Akeem

1) How do you feel about kids? Do you have kids? Do you want kids? Why or why not? Be honest.

_____

_____

_____

_____

_____

_____

_____

_____

_____

CHAPTER 9- ROEMELO AND PRINCE AKEEM (continued)

2) What is your worst moment of motherhood? Most embarrassing? Most joyful?

_____

_____

_____

_____

_____

_____

_____

_____

_____

_____

_____

_____

_____

_____

_____

_____

_____

_____

CHAPTER 9- ROEMELO AND PRINCE AKEEM (continued)

3) How do you feel about your parenting style? What do you need to do more of?

_____
_____
_____
_____
_____
_____
_____
_____
_____
_____
_____
_____
_____
_____
_____
_____
_____
_____
_____

CHAPTER 9- ROEMELO AND PRINCE AKEEM (continued)

4) Do you enjoy parenthood, or is it a strain?

Write to God about how you feel and see what He has to say.

_____

_____

_____

_____

_____

_____

_____

_____

_____

_____

_____

_____

_____

_____

_____

CHAPTER 9- ROEMELO AND PRINCE AKEEM (continued)

5) Have you ever had an abortion? How does it make you feel? Do you receive the forgiveness of God?

_____

_____

_____

_____

_____

_____

_____

_____

_____

_____

_____

_____

_____

_____

_____

_____

_____

CHAPTER 9- ROEMELO AND PRINCE AKEEM (continued)

6) Have you ever had a miscarriage? Have you discussed with God your feelings about that tragedy? Write to Him about it. Be vulnerable.

_____

_____

_____

_____

_____

_____

_____

_____

_____

_____

_____

_____

_____

_____

_____

_____

_____

_____

CHAPTER 9- ROEMELO AND PRINCE AKEEM (continued)

7) What are your hopes and dreams for your children? What is your commitment to their growth, development, and well-being?

_____

_____

_____

_____

_____

_____

_____

_____

_____

_____

_____

_____

_____

_____

_____

_____

_____

CHAPTER 9- ROEMELO AND PRINCE AKEEM (continued)

8) Write an individual letter to each of your children and give it to them one day. Watch God bless your relationship.

_____

_____

_____

_____

_____

_____

_____

_____

_____

_____

_____

_____

_____

_____

_____

_____

_____

_____

Prayer Reflection-Chapter 9

Prayer Reflection

Use this page to write a prayer or listen to what God is saying to you in this chapter.

_____

_____

_____

_____

_____

_____

_____

Scripture Reflection-
Chapter 9

Scripture Reflection

Use these scriptures for deeper reflection, prayer, and revelation.

- *Psalm 127:3 – Children are a gift from the Lord.*

- *Proverbs 22:6 – Train up a child in the way he should go.*

- *Isaiah 40:11 – He gently leads those with young.*

Scripture Reflection-Chapter 9 (continued)

Scripture Reflection (continued)

Use these scriptures for deeper reflection, prayer, and revelation.

- *Jeremiah 29:11 – I know the plans I have for you.*

- *Isaiah 49:15, 16 – Can a mother forget her child?*

Chapter 10

This Black Girl Doesn't Do Magic

1) Have you had a near-death experience? What do you remember about that moment? Write about it.

_____

_____

_____

_____

_____

_____

_____

_____

_____

THIS BLACK GIRL DOESN'T DO MAGIC (continued)

2) What do you want people to remember about you when you leave this world? What do you want the Heavenly Father to say about you when you meet Him face-to-face?

_____

_____

_____

_____

_____

_____

_____

_____

_____

_____

_____

_____

_____

_____

THIS BLACK GIRL DOESN'T DO MAGIC (continued)

3) Do you understand who you are? Does your understanding of who you are come from God or the world? Be honest.

_____

_____

_____

_____

_____

_____

_____

_____

_____

_____

_____

_____

_____

_____

_____

_____

_____

_____

_____

THIS BLACK GIRL DOESN'T DO MAGIC (continued)

4) Are you clear about what you believe? Do you feel solid about your faith that when you pass away, you know where you will spend eternity? If not, how can you get reassured?

_____

_____

_____

_____

_____

_____

_____

_____

_____

_____

_____

_____

_____

THIS BLACK GIRL DOESN'T DO MAGIC (continued)

5) What leads you? Is it your emotions? Your trauma? Your appetite? The Holy Spirit? Your mind? Write about it.

_____

_____

_____

_____

_____

_____

_____

_____

_____

_____

_____

_____

_____

_____

_____

_____

_____

THIS BLACK GIRL DOESN'T DO MAGIC (continued)

6) What parts of you are you ready to let go of? What are you struggling to let go of? Write to the Lord about it.

_____

_____

_____

_____

_____

_____

_____

_____

_____

_____

_____

_____

_____

_____

_____

_____

_____

_____

THIS BLACK GIRL DOESN'T DO MAGIC (continued)

7) Write a letter to the Most High Savior and King, thanking Him for His sacrifice on the cross.

_____

_____

_____

_____

_____

_____

_____

_____

_____

_____

_____

_____

_____

_____

_____

_____

_____

THIS BLACK GIRL DOESN'T DO MAGIC (continued)

8) Pray for yourself. Spend some time listening to The Holy Spirit.

Write a letter to your new self. Encourage them. Tell your new self what to do next.

Say hello to the new you!

_____

_____

_____

_____

_____

_____

_____

_____

_____

_____

_____

_____

Prayer Reflection- Chapter 10

Prayer Reflection

Use this page to write a prayer or listen to what God is saying to you in this chapter.

_____

_____

_____

_____

_____

_____

_____

_____

Scripture Reflection-
Chapter 10

Scripture Reflection

Use these scriptures for deeper reflection, prayer, and revelation.

- *Hebrews 9:27 – People are destined to die once, and after that...*

- *Deuteronomy 18:10–12 – Do not practice sorcery or witchcraft.*

- *John 14:6 – I am the way, the truth, and the life.*

Scripture Reflection-Chapter 10 (continued)

Scripture Reflection (continued)

Use these scriptures for deeper reflection, prayer, and revelation.

- *2 Timothy 4:7, 8 – I have fought the good fight...*

- *Revelation 21:4 – He will wipe away every tear.*

About the Author

Sharelle McNair is a bold and passionate teacher of the Gospel, speaker, and creative based in Richmond, Virginia. A devoted mother of two sons, Sharelle uses her many gifts to serve God across multiple ministries with an unapologetic voice for truth, healing, and identity in Christ.

Although she grew up attending church, Sharelle's true faith journey began after the tragic loss of her cousin to a drug overdose in 2009. That pivotal moment led her to surrender her life to Christ and begin a transformative walk toward sanctification and purpose. Her testimony is one of resilience, grace, and revelation—walking through pain, identity loss, and cultural deception to discover who she truly is in God.

She currently serves as an Executive Leader, Gospel Teacher, Intercessor, and Music Curator at Transformed City Church under the leadership of Pastors Brad and Quiana Johnson. Sharelle is also an organizer and assistant for the Unquenchable Worshippers Dance Team, where she uses music and movement to minister the freedom of Christ.

Known for her raw, relatable, and refreshingly real style, Sharelle has spoken at numerous conferences, women's events, and podcasts, using her story to help others break free from worldly labels and reclaim their God-given identity.

Beyond ministry, she finds joy in cultural festivals, dancing to music, exploring fashion through her signature earrings, and having deep conversations over mimosas with friends. Her heart beats for laughter, healing, sisterhood, and creating spaces where even the outcasts feel the love of Christ.

Her life and ministry are grounded in Colossians 3:16–17 (NLT), a reminder to live as a representative of Jesus in everything she does.

"Let the message about Christ, in all its richness, fill your lives... And whatever you do or say, do it as a representative of the Lord Jesus, giving thanks through him to God the Father."

Connect with Sharelle:

info@sharellemcnair.com

www.sharellemcnair.com

Also by Sharelle McNair

If this journal has stirred something in you, don't stop here—read the book that started it all. In *Goodbye Gemini: Reclaiming My Identity. Finding The Truth*, Sharelle McNair shares the raw, powerful story that inspired this journal and invites you to discover your true identity in Christ. Your healing journey isn't complete without it.

www.ingramcontent.com/pod-product-compliance
Lightning Source LLC
Chambersburg PA
CBHW051209120626

46547CB00013B/1277